TIDAL

TIDAL

JOSH KALSCHEUR

FOUR WAY BOOKS
TRIBECA

for my parents

Please direct all inquiries to:
Editorial Office
Four Way Books
POB 535, Village Station
New York, NY 10014
www.fourwaybooks.com

Library of Congress Cataloging-in-Publication Data

Kalscheur, Josh.
[Poems. Selections]
Tidal / Josh Kalscheur.
pages cm
ISBN 978-1-935536-53-6 (alk. paper)
I. Title.
PS3611.A456T53 2014
811'.6--dc23
                    2014030214

Funding for this book was provided in part by a generous donation
in memory of John J. Wilson.

CONTENTS

III

"*Just north of the equator in the western Pacific, strung out over nearly three thousand miles, lay the islands of the Caroline and Marshall groups. The term Micronesia, which came to be used to designate these groups and their neighboring archipelagoes, suits them well, for the islands are no more than tiny specks in a two-million-square-mile expanse of ocean . . .*"

Francis X. Hezel, S.J.
The First Taint of Civilization, 1983

EXPLANATION

The liquor-stand boy said it started when rocks flew from a breadfruit,
when it was still windy, but the girls parsing their hair for lice
say no way, there were two of them, and their pants were down

same as always. The blanket was clean on one side. The one dog
whose vagina hangs loose and bleeds, barked the whole time.
The goiter dog might be dead. That's what the kids say who were playing

with the brake pads of a broken car. The uncles drank yeast
and Asahi and sang those songs about home. Their sons
agreed and dented an oil barrel with rebar and pig bones.

The rusted satellite dish echoed the sound. The boy who speaks
good English says a gun is buried by the cookhouse,
next to where the thighs bleed out. The one who works

the Dirty Curve told a man bullets are only for slingshots.
That explains it. The mothers say no one screams like that.
It was more of a muffle. The volleyball net was tangled

and ripped open. The man with scars and big ears
insists the house with the warrior masks shook.
The painted names on the Japanese tank bled, but the high titles

won't look to the cliff. They speak the old language and spit. The rain
factors in somehow, and the green clouds hanging over Mabuchi Hill.
The gas-sniffer shakes his head at the cage hut where four men play pool.

Follow the bleached rat-tail, says the unmarried woman. If he holds
anything in his hands, don't look at the fat of his face. Forget
what she says and follow the trail of batteries to the rail ties,

5

says the boy who boys call a fag. Maybe they took the two a.m.
to Guam. The aunties wonder what will happen in the taro patch.
It could be worse with a gas can or vines. The order of things

makes a difference. The girl with the burned face says so, she wants this
piece by piece. She says men will come when the hibiscus
ropes dry, and when they point and pick it all up, the prayers are done.

VISTA

Something in the fire falling over the road
at this hour, the riot-high flames spreading light
over Sapuk at dusk, laid-flat husks turning to dust,

men yelling discreetly *it might move or go higher*,
water catchments like pots whistling to boil,
the whole compound setting itself into a sort of haze,

a mirage of half-lit houses clouded, some foreign fog
rolling into the cookhouses, something in the settling ash
in the coconut trees, into the window frames

of flattened flatbeds, the blocked-out peak of Tol.
At this height maybe nothing will reach us,
maybe the trash pile from a cousin's land, debris

shredded in the trade winds, sparks from slacked
power lines arcing from village to village, bursting
at the busted generator boxes, the gathered air buzzing

to a blackened pitch, the clustered piles of dead coral
thrown to the heat, the pressured hum and singe
heard in the pandanus, the faces still quiet when it climbs

to a dying plumeria branch, the women beginning to laugh
in the ears of their daughters, twisting loose their braids,
the boys running in circles they draw in the dirt.

JAIL BY CHURCH AND SCHOOL

You too might find yourself
dragged from the dock by men
with plastic badges, someone's blood drying
on your legs, a smile cut into your knee.
You too might be chained to a beam
in the main room with embezzlers
and frauds, still-stupored taro thieves,
the one Mormon practicing
in the corner with a broken sling-shot,
the infected and fevered addicts
who beat their women
but not to death. It's a full lot tonight
and the guard nods from sleep
then lets the nearly sober go, the cripples
and quiet crazies, the almost dead
choking to breathe, the sad boys
who dream their fathers still pray
for them in the village, on the road,
when they stalk the shoreline
for sleeping fish. The radio plays
a creed in the melody of Amazing Grace.
In the two real cells with real bars
are rapists who fucked the wrong girls,
the high-title daughters and pure-bloods,
the best-dressed girls from Guam.
You too might learn the truth of the turtle
and the low tide, matters of the heart
gone dark. There's a story the men tell
where they take you to the top
of a hill and make you kneel
and recite the sacred words

of the mountainside. You climb
a tree with a rope and jump
like you want nothing else
but to die in that holiness.
You too should imagine the echoed
grind, the sleepless lean, the long drop,
the flies and tree-rats filling
your mouth, eating your bones
to nothing.

NIGHTCRAWL

The night I touch you on the back
of my brother's flatbed after the men pull
the cord and the smoke thins to nothing.

The aftermath of the feast
when the boys hit maría straight off the stem
and shred Gem Clear bottlenecks

to thin strips, tying them into rings
and wristbands. I think of nothing
when the girls pick up plumerias

they dropped during the stomp dance.
They undo their hair braid by braid
but I think of nothing. I won't look at you now

but know the path you might take.
I know it's nowhere near time
to start singing. I know you'll loop a finger

through the thatch in your basket.
You might find a comb or a bottle of oil.
I know how this goes. If I hear anything,

it's the small plane's single engine going above
the bare rock on Wittapong. I have no right
to be here. You'll walk barefoot

when you circle your way to my side.
We have until the tide pulls away
to finish what you started.

PROMISE BROTHER

I want to tell you something.
The boy with lined eyes
hid by a rusted pole and scraped it

so I heard. His sister's shirt
was unbuttoned around his chest
and his nails stained red

with betelnut spit.
I didn't know his father's name.
He stripped a rice bag

in his hand. I watched him
weave the strands and loop
them tight. He left clouds

where his weight had pressed
and turned the ground to dust.
I could hear my mother in the village

cutting the heads for soup
and dropping the tails in lard.
His mouth was round, like it came

from the face of a bigger man.
The outboard motors churned
the shallow water when boats

came to shore. I turned my back
and his shadow cut me
into the mangrove trees.

The colors went from gray
to black, depending on the sun,
depending on the shapes

of the vines and the angles
we made of our bodies.

EXPLANATION

The girl from Cottage Grove went too far
this time, but swears it was just harmonies
with him, with the only local hymn

she knew by heart, but he says
there are reasons for his hat hanging
by the stairs, his ring caught

in her window-wire. Now
his single cousins stalk the causeway,
say their chance will come

to climb the hill. Even the home priest
props papaya plants with anvils
and flattens half the road

with gravel, waters it down
with his one working hose.
Even the women weaving palms

needle fish-ribs in the dirt
when the white girls jog a route
they barely know, past the blue house

with rows of spears spared
from the shrinking shore. Maybe
she touched a vein that made her

nipples grow. In the floating homes
the story goes that a metal post
scratched her tile and in Fefan

the floor rattled. In Tol he tied her
lavalava and left marks. In Sapuk
the few thin women want proof

he barely breathed, that geckos fell
from the cabinets. And the oldest sons
hear and Nepukos hears, Mwan,

Uman, the plugged wells, the splintered
dock posts and gutted huts, the culled
quarry, the last cathedral with glass.

Maybe there were magnums
and a hand pulling him in.
Maybe the men with nightsticks

tease grass with their teeth
when a white girl runs by
jingling two shots of mace

on her hip. Maybe they tell a story
of a skirt unthreading itself,
how it made a trail in the scaling

vines, in the lighter shadows
that settle in the bed of a tree.

GIRL FROM TONOAS

How sadness seated itself in the meetinghouse,
the synthesizer fuzz humming a ring into the mesh-wire walls,
flies looming on fish bones after the feast, mosquitoes fighting
the generator flicker, the church group girls folding their skirts
to a hula roll at the hip, the staccato treble beginning to swing,
the girl with the burned face in front, her center scars staring,
the marks corroded even in the lips, the joints' circled pop moving
in unison along the troupe, the ripple of skin lighter on the cheek curves,
symmetry designing itself there, the fixed foreheads turning, the low note
dip of the slick chin, strict angles forming fissures, the skirt
slowing subtle on the low bass pulse, how it must've been grease
in the cookhouse or heat wind off the earth oven, peeled
pressure passing, spotted hands spiraled over the head, the pirouette
pouring down the shoulder, throbbing steady in the sweat-line,
the crescendo quarter-notes scoring wrinkles, faults severed
in the baggy eye-skin, waves undulant parabola under jawbone,
the soirée lofted elbows, a brush of deep knees bending sacred
to the floor, the leaning men on the walls, the wept women
whirling towels, on the head the hair falling halfway
to the calf muscles, how the hips must crack in the final shake,
down the sinew pulled to a secluded stretch, sweeping
strokes caught in the floor-cracks, the codified sighs constrained,
air rendered to a nondescript steam, until the gas fizzles
to reverbs of light, and the darkness spreads itself.

SARAM

The moon drew a line through the doors
to where we sat. We faced forward
to the statues, and I scratched my name

into the knob of pew dividing us.
Where my hips sat my skirt billowed
out. You tapped your toes into the kneeler

and left a mark. There was nobody there
to revise the silence, its stark incense
passing sweetly through. Only the anonymous echo

of an animal beat into the concrete
beneath us. The air grew boggy
in your hands. I could see it in the tremor

of your wrists, how the heart beat itself out
on the inside of your arm. You flicked
a lighter on and off. I wondered how your hand

might curl if it fisted, or how the knuckles
might go soft in my palms. When you looked
to the orange wall behind the crucifix,

I let my hair fall. The hush it made
when it flooded from the comb
sounded like breath. The knots of wood

we leaned on loosened. The coconut oil slicked
a sheen to the bench. What you held
and passed from finger to finger

I didn't know. Something like steps
moved from aisle to aisle. The hair puddled
into the sides of our knees. It grew darker there

when the clouds piled onto each other.
We looked forward and huddled.
The pews ached with the shift of our weight.

VOYEURS

In the heated banter near Sapuk School
my brothers huddled

in half-moons around it
watching the flat section of the road

the flex of hip thrusted
the mocked act

crowded mutt males working inverses
in the body's softest underskin

a rattle echoing the wire-grate window
the jolt of knee-bends rubbing

a burn running through thigh sinew
dogs marking a beat down

ten-litter teats dragging a fog-dust
a rooted chorus

a quarter-terrier's thudded weight
the speckle-gray half-hound

moping the foreground
the weaker breeds bleeding from the ears

submissive in the dense heat
the dogs going for it

under the mango tree
the thought my brothers must drum

in the sporadic head-turns
the tightening calves

how pain must enter somewhere
shift indifferently

even the flies flocking to the bloodspot
the blurred swarm settling.

GRIEVANCE

*Open House with Madam Ambassador Miriam Hughes, the U.S.
Ambassador to FSM from September 2007 to September 2009, at
Hard Wreck Café*

Here you are on the fifth day of rain with the lights cut,
wires siphoned to useless plugs in storefronts,
fried filament swinging by hibiscus, the cat-eyed
kero-lamps blinking, and Madam, these days teeter
the cratered corners, quicksand graveled ponds
shaded to shit, fecal palettes foaming in ditches,
fuming and strewn, perfumed to cesspools
and dissolved ribs of rebar. And this is nothing.
Think of the manhole geysers lifted over roadside kids
who trail chickens, biscuit tins, barefoot or slippered,
the slivered open-boils, cryptosporidium pooling
in the potholes, leptospirosis rivered weakly like blood
from a congested heart, and that movement,
it pains you, that tepid vapor, the beetled film scattered
to spores, the congenital silence flat-lining the night
in Parem. And I know the unattended sores bubbled
in shingle ridges, char-marks like smoked meat,
leprous slits in the skin, pestilential flesh patched
to mats, to flecks left pussing and nothing much else
defines how this feels, how you keep sweeping out
what pours in, what churns the dock water
on the thirtieth day blacked out, puffed out
in the cheeks and swollen in folds under the eyes,
stricken to conditioned twitches at any tic of light,
any satellite flash perforating the storm-front,
any spark falling to frays in the road.

THROWDOWN

The buzz comes from the baseline and the rubble border
to the jungle, here at the village's one standing rim,
the only cement left with lines. Even the boys hitting short shots
know to hold up, shirtless in the midday sun, even the girls
stop at three notches in nearby trees, the washed-up drunks
jacking threes grow still, let their misses trail off in the high grass.
They know him by the shadows off his shoulders, straight
from the Guam Rec leagues, the legend of cracked backboards
and splintered posts, blow-bys and blocked shots
to the bleachers, basking in the crowds rubbing dust-clouds
in the windy seasons, the air-ball swishes at the no-net courts of Tol,
the half-quiet girls toeing the patched grass, staring, lonely
for no one. Here he dribbles twice to his left
and loops a no-look pass to himself, and if there's a word
for the curves he made, the arc and degrees of space
in his wake, lost in the launch of it all, there was enough jump
under the palms of his feet for all the rolling eyes,
all the bandannas flapping while he rushed break-neck
to the basket, the rock grinding to a halt on the touch
before takeoff, higher than any man, poster-high,
ladder-high, higher than their fathers' hands, cupped on his forearm
and cocked like a neck about to bite, the ball ripping
over the rim with sprays of rust-flecks and rotted wood
as a reverb of grunts makes its way in waves,
and all the boys stand up, all the almost-dunkers,
all the finger-tip rim touchers, the stilted wrists and lead feet,
all the stomping ones, the finesse boys with not-enough ups
or the right kicks, all the tall ones with no hops,
all the jammed-thumbs, they all watch the ball's slow roll
in the gravel, the endless mud from potholes never patched,

praising the last bounces, a motion hanging muggy
in the air, seeing the ball lean from lace to lace,
still spinning and not stopping—

EXPLANATION

I slung rocks into the roadside mango tree,
at the rotted clumps aching to drop what was too sweet
to hold any longer. I played my ukulele
and the strings broke. I sat and watched you.
The engine in the truck you rode whined
to a stall. Let me tell you this had nothing to do
with your thighs or the chewed pulp-red betelnut
wedged in your cheek, spat like a sickness
into the jungle. You'd come this way before,
a turtle shell comb lodged in your hair, singing
acappella. You think I wanted to fuck you,
lead you to some concrete showerhouse and sing
a love song into the blossom tucked behind your ear?
It's true. You could've raised your eyebrows
and meant yes. You could've tugged on your skirt
for the men at the corner. I stripped a ukulele string,
sacrificed the neck, lobbed a mango your way.
It wouldn't fall but floated to the cliff above
the road, sweeping down and cutting wings
into its skin. It flew back to its branch. It looked past
where I sat on the carcass of a Honda, past the sway
of banana leaf, to the wall of mud behind me
and up the striated wall to the cliff again. It waited
for the ocean to sing to the shore, for exhaust to gray
in the sky and disappear. And then it fell softly
into the wind, the trail of juice and flies running after,
buzzing and catching in the braids of your hair.

GOOD AND CLEAN

With a wet towel drawn across my back,
massaged into me
in the motion of his knowing,
I know more is meant for me
in the way more is expected for a man of God.

He says I'm his first
and I tell him he's the first man I've taken
to the point of disappearing.
Even now I have an idea about the beginning
and the end of temperance.

In the flatbed I'm handed two plugs
to cut my gums and the skin inside my cheeks
to bleeding. The orders are clear
and I finish a joke he starts
about a man with no arms or legs

rolling himself into the ocean.
When we are hungry I rip a piece of breadfruit
in two. When he laughs it is my time
to laugh, and when he stops I know his home
is mine for the time being.

We begin to move through the curves
of the road and turn left down a stretch
we both know so well we could almost
close our eyes and lean from the shore
to the jungle, one edge to the other.

CREATION MYTH

A woman calling herself God
hangs in heaven.
From the light she grips
she cuts three boys, three sharp-rocked
beginnings. She wraps the reef around them,
she holds the water until they begin to grow
their shores. Birds from her hands
find what is sweet is not always
alive. From her sky
ribbed clouds go nowhere
the boys think. She becomes a shadow
when they want darkness. She becomes
a residue of heat they clean
from their breadfruit trees. It is sad, she knows,
but good, to want them scattered,
secluded, these incidents of light.

II

PROVISIONS

Always this grinding out another afternoon
near the abandoned Japanese rail ties, waiting
for the boys to gather, always this leaving Iras
at three from the meetinghouse with our backs
to the road, steeplechasing the flatbed
through the monsoon-grooved pot hole lakes
still shin-deep after a month without rain,
the wheeled ripple of oil-slicked silt splashing up

to the doors, the cadre of kids plodding the mangrove
with machetes and slingshots, chickens tied to ropes
like pets, ribbed mutts sulking, the dirge-slow cruise
into Nepukos, always like this on a payday in April,
at TTC, Shigeto's, in Asa where everything comes
in cases or sacks, in the lowly-lit aisled zōri chaos,
where on Friday the State's Compact funds trickle
down, the late-day waiting with five fifty-pound bags

of Guam Rose, three stacks of Triple Three Mackerel
with oil, soft bones like fried noodles, Yamasa
soy sauce in two-liter handled jugs, square tins
of Argentina corned beef off the ship from Darwin,
the locked gelatinous settling of lard, Aji-No-Moto
in the bulk bags they don't sell anywhere but stateside
oriental joints. Here we are sweating it out in the loadup
with flats of Chinese colas, Black Label luncheon

slabbed into side supports, with the pwi pwis,
the mwasamwas weight of a dozen cartons
of the super-pasteurized, the sweetened condensed
Carnation glaze, the sun beating a syrupy film

29

into the rubber-patched steering wheel, the sniffing gas men
stalking shade and the bent benches, the blackened
women selling rotten ropes of tapioca tin-wrapped
for whites, warmer than anything in our bodies,

everything not fresh from China, or Japan with the pirated
yellow-fins, sold back headless in cuts of Amerikana
fillet, mashed to a puck-sized pulp, the turkey tail
not considered fit for food in the states, the fat gristling
down, the FDA-reject giblets scraped from the Perdue
live-kill rooms, twenty-five quartered California thighs
and legs, Iowa pig bile thawed to a mucus, fresh
from the docks with corners rat-pocked from the float over,

Korean Kimchee in the glass bottles, as fancy as you get
this equatorial, this far nowhere, these festering Pacific
pimples, detritus specks of mistakes with spray-painted
governmental signs, the sputtering hope in the monthly
Mobil ship, these ramshackle ghetto remnants
of Honolulu, this island of the Compact State, the eroded
aid of the Trust Territory era, ten-year-old vendors
of single cigarettes, stacking the Filipino pancit up

past the window, squares like blocks of C-rations,
blind spots moving with the sloped border of the jungle,
the derelict dust rising for the first time since the bowels
of the Chief Mailo, ratcheting the stick into any gear
that'll move this much weight, and we're not
the only ones with cases of Red Horse and fifths
of Gem Clear, the prim single travelers of Fleischmann's
for the road, bags of puu and lime to cut the cheeks,

the stinging nic-hit of Salem in the lips, drive it back
to where it started and pound down another for whoever
goes stoning the pickups with the tinted windows
and wailer lights black-marketed from Hilo, always like this,
families of land plotted out like this, on the roadside
the same muted emptiness sitting on the Dirty Curve
before Sapuk, nothing left in the flickering end of gas
in the compound generator, and never anything

lighting this place but the trash fires, or stirred
fluorescence in the tin-lid cut shores, going bright
in only the heavy slaps of tide, fighting to get the light
out, sparking a copra husk in the used oil barrel rusted
to a sieve, cranking the wick up the kerosene lamps,
searching the mountain grass going clear in the first hour
of moonlight, always like this, how it grows articulately
in the cloudless night, blade to blade a blend of them

trading angles in the wind, it's all enough to lie down
and strain for, to sit rigid and wait in the vine-thick air.

REMITTANCE

In October when the banks cave and they hike rice
to forty a sack, the slack-jaws in Grand Rapids catch flak
in phone calls and swear to pitch in their Bissell severance.
Then the blue shirts in Tulsa pool a grand from Pell Grants
and pledge their injury comp whenever it kicks in.
And the short skirts in Little Rock slip fifties in flat rates
and cut what they can from their wills. In October
the freight from Guam slows when crude goes

through the roof. The Portland third-shifts punch holes
in pleather coats and post crates to Chuuk, and the motel ladies
drum up quick cash for the first time. In Baltimore
it's scratch-offs and forged checks, and in Waco
it's toner-streaked tens, and in the sub-parish,
on the paved side of the hill, the pink-skin cloak keeps
the cause with sick visits and vigils. The loincloths
kneel on the Waikiki strip gripping paper cups.

And it's like this in Oklahoma City where the welding rods fade
from a brighter shade, and it's like this in Salt Lake
with the shelf-stocking crews, like the dock water flooding
the junked-out boats and smearing the rocks slick
when ships from Saipan pull to port, and still, these mornings
keep stacking up with men hawking golf balls
at flea markets, and the mail slots still bulge in the lightless
post room, and the muumuus tighten like kites

in the trade winds, off the reef edge, far from Carson City,
from Tacoma, from Tempe, from every town surrounding
Santa Fe, every interstate ramp-napper off I-80 to Denver,
every brick-layer, every telemarketer scraping away

the fake lamps of the industrial parks, every boy trolling
the road, three-deep, resigned to a sort of circled trance.
These are the fathers, the distant cousins, these are the last
elders, the other brothers who bear the brunt of it.

ENLISTMENT

Guam, U.S.A

All the people not from here, all the Texan lilt
temp jobs, all the mirage of massage parlors, knock-off
Vegas gigs, B-stars wasted on Hilton buffets, Hummer-drunk
joyrides, the camo and coded chatter of terminal
hops to Hawaii, per diems splurged on hijacked handicrafts, bastard
myth images, one-day jaunts, layover benders, Duty Free
Marlb-Red cartons, all the billboarded faux-nesians and fast-cash stands
at luggage lines, plastic bags groaning, the fattened waddling
and shop-worn heels toeing too-new curbs on the vacant strip
in Agana. All the knicked-chin boys at the Andersen Base,
all from Michigan from towns no one says they're from,
all the shock of palm trees and brown strippers, Chamorras
waiting tables in the *Hafa Adai* strip mall, clinging
to fat-lipped foreign sounds, loitering with forties in a pawn shop,
waiting for wind with a borrowed board by the landing strip, revving
a rented bike on the up-curve to Two Lover's Point, to the bent guard rails'
sheer drop, here *Where America's Day Begins,* the set flares pushing off
the burnt clouds passing for sunset, they pretend to pull clips,
they kill birds and watch them fall.

A FAIR DEAL

A pack of good weed seeds and ten pounds of rice
I give you for a fair price. Three bags of copra
and fresh tuna meat I weigh and wrap for you.
I know what a dollar is worth
stateside, in your trumped-up markets.
I've been to the city of LA.
I've drunk your coffee sugarless
with no cream. I know what it means
to mean business, what a shook hand has to do
with bravado and pressure, what proud posture
has to do with a living wage. I know your eye contact,
your uniforms with pockets embroidered with cursive.
I'm fluent in small-talk, the well-off and worldly
dialect. I've played the barely-getting-by
and slept under a roof. I've played a swindler
with a fake Latino accent who spits something red
from his mouth. If I give you local chicken and tapioca,
a month's worth packed in ice and portioned,
will you give me a license for a gun and a flight to Majuro?
Will you find me an airport job wrapping boxes with tape?
I can give you turtleshell combs on the side.
I've been a gentleman once in my life.
I'll give you golden cowries and the roots
of pepper plants, and you'll give me your luggage.
I know where you're going once you leave here
and where you're coming from.
I've walked in those leather shoes before
and the road felt unreal under my feet.

RAVE

The room where we dance.
The room with pool cues
and eight-balls, lights that last
a brown-out, lights we stole
from the runway. The room
with posts we swing from.
The culture we designed
bends tonight, we shake our hips at it.
There are people touching
for the first time who love
each other. Women dragging boys
on the floor when the music settles
to an even beat, a bass-laid trance.
Women shotgunning Red Horse
who tomorrow will meet their husbands
on the road. Anyone can come here
if they sing the right words.
Anyone can come
if they flash a piece of ivory nut.
We paint our lips red and kiss
the women we know will love
the mark it makes
in the clouded moonlight,
the cracks in the thatch.
Where do we go from here
except against the wall
with our hands over our heads?
The boys ready their sticks
and red cloths.
The turtle we pray to
sings what he sings and that's enough.

EXPLANATION

Now the mother drains two cups of pus
from three heads on her daughter's chest.
The half-moon wound wrinkles and rolls

and throbs, heart-like. The redder skin ripples
to a scab at the shoulders. The towels turn
yellow and hot like shore water. A TB sign

and a chain hang from the hospital door.
The mother finds fishbones, leaves to fan
her face, a boy to swat flies and stand

over sores on her feet. She tells him to
pray. The Peace Corps blonde picks Cipro
and sterile pads from the floor. Fingertips go

numb and puff and curl. They move
on their own. The healer sings between the road
and the water, moving her hands like a paddle

lost in the spin of a wave. It's simple. In Sapuk,
in the blossoms of vines behind the hill, the healer
opens two stems and squeezes the liquid clear.

The forearms speckle first. A cloth covers the ground
where the path once was. Her breath shrills
into the meetinghouse. The road fills with men.

MERCY SHIP

Here come the uniformed men with their cargo
and clean needles, their jackhammers and plaster bags,
their steel supports, drill bits and provisional masks
packed in airless crates, their locked guns tucked
in their belts, driving their big engines, their American
trucks in a convoy to the State Hospital, the trauma
center and TB ward, leper colony and insane asylum,
the HIV unit where there's a man no one touches.
Here they come with sterile gloves and test kits,
the strict measures of chain-of-command charts,
stripping the floor in the main hall and bleaching
dim rooms and broom closets, check-marking forms
for tainted blood, staph-soaked scalpels and towels,
soiled hands, faulty doorknobs and doctors
who should quit. Here they come tearing down walls
eaten to nothing by termites, promising to build them
again with boards of foreign wood. Here they come
through Mwan with their pink-tinted triceps
and tattoos, their buzz-cuts freshly groomed
from time in Guam, tossing quarters and dimes
to the shirtless boy running at second-gear speed
through the road, dodging potholes and mackerel cans,
slapping a handprint on the back-hatch, yelling
bombs away, bombs away, bombs away.

REGIMENT, 1941

We dig up stalks of corn and feed the pigs
until their stomachs explode. We march
in rows and close our eyes to show them
we've learned. Hold a shotgun steady,
arch your back, they say from a megaphone,
in a tower they cut from breadfruit wood,
through a window with bars. We shoot
the wounded mutts on command
in the head. There's a man whose name is written
in symbols over his pocket, who tells us
to burn the hillside, and we do, for practice,
with the wind at our backs. We wait in a bunker
to watch for what moves through the smoke.
This is how the shoulder rotates to throw
a grenade, and they make the motion.
Here is a field of rice paddies we built
by flooding the taro swamp. Here is the temple
where we poured the mold of Buddha.
Here is how to point a gun to a plane's window
and shatter it. On the island of Tonoas
we cull the vines and roots where concrete
will cover the clay and become a nerve center.
This is the word for road. This is a Jeep,
they teach the girls. There are ways to ride them
without falling. This is how to stop a thigh
from bleeding when shrapnel gashes deep
and disappears. There are ways to kill fish
we didn't know and ways to hold a knife
to the gills. We bury pipes and wires
and learn codes meaning hide, find cover,
load your guns and fire, bury yourself

wherever you are. We learn the sounds
for a dying propeller and the whistle,
the endless spiral. On the far shore of Etten,
we invent a runway from dead coral we stack
and from a village we flatten with tanks.

LOW BUDGET MICHAEL

First I stalk them with a pinhole
from the dive-shop to the Presidential Suite
where I prop a tripod on a block of wood
in the corner. This is their first time
and they need teaching. She's a big girl
and I tell her to shake her ass so it blurs
in the camera lens like a wind-up toy.
They laugh too much so I tell them
to shut up. His dick has folds of skin
like an older man. I tell him to strap on
a gorilla mask and then to dribble spit
through the mouth-hole so it drips down
to the ground. I want the old classics,
him with the Chuukese hammer,
her with cuts in her arms, quiet puffs
of sound in the camera mic, the real look
of her eyes filling up like she might cry
happy tears. I used to love when screams
popped through the screen and maxed out
and went silent. It could surprise you.
It could get you to jump from your chair.
The little room, the bleached lighting,
the old sticky traps stacked halfway
to the ceiling, a red cloth tossed on the mat.
Saying, put your hand here, bend this way,
crawl like this, close to the nails,
until the skin turns raw. There are girls
I've had with long, braided hair
hanging to the ground, ready for anything.
There are girls I'd get to the compound
drunk on tubâ, who'd come to the jungle,

and we'd duck the shadows of taro leaves,
watch the moon die behind the reef
and their gold teeth would glow.
This is their first time so I let them hug.
I let them kiss with just their lips.
I tell them I'm rolling but I'm not.
I tell them to almost smile, to twist
their faces together so they touch.

STATESIDE

He could be the B-flick brown body, the stand-in
peace-pipe, the Navajo deadbeat chaining Pall Malls,
blocked from scene to scene. He could be the caddie kid
Chicano in California after free drinks and swing tips,
the dead ringer Inuit, the flea market scammer courting
fat folks with rolls of quarters flicked from ear to ear.
He could be the troubled child, the reservation
redneck extra. He could be the magic man, the one-trick-pony
flipping jacks to queens, cutting a gut through a false
wall, the strings spliced with claps and snaps of the finger.
He's got those knee-deep braids, those Malay eyes,
those half-words, that soft-flesh face. He could
trapeze. He could circus. He could jump from rung
to rung. He could circuit the fairs, bellow echoes
through conch shells. He could stick dance
and loincloth the park, his jellyfish scar lined from thigh
to thigh. He could high-rise paint with pails
of slum lord blue. He could shingle and scrape,
he could slip from step to step. He could dangle
with a rag scaling the sky-scraped tinteds,
the condo sky-lights. He could be part-time,
some-time, any-time at the Porta-Potty place,
any grape-picking plantation off the interstate,
any third shift at the Matson plant lifting boxes,
any chance to sound out a sign at the eight-way stop.
He could be the accented radio ad. He could be the animated
borders of his body. He could bed-pan, he could plasma,
he could blast from town to town, cityscape to plains.
He could be thundercloud, the weak-kneed man,
the clawed-finger, the shuffled and herded, the courier,

the undone, a taxi man at the station, lost in the noise
of his voice, the ticks and the beat of it, the words
in his mouth meaning come with me.

CONTINENTAL

Before we fly to Fort Benning
my brother and I buy a case of Asahi
and set up shop in a spot with barely
even a tree, down by the tire-fixing place
near a stream feeding out to the lagoon,
getting drunk before the beer tastes like piss.
We aim wads of betelnut at rats darting
from a pipe, maxi pads in their mouths.
We know what's going on. We march
in place and cock-eye a salute
to the spray-painted sign of the bank.
We imagine our bodies sprawled
across a back page ad, our nipples
like bulletheads. We imagine our photos
at the Guam airport, blown up and framed
in the lobby, the glitter of the clicking signs
shining over them, our skin smooth
with coconut oil, full-colored with camo-green
and brown, the berets set straight,
the backdrop flag crisp. We make those faces
like we might choke and then we laugh
our heads off. I put my finger in the top
of a pipe and my brother points
at the run-down shack near the jungle.
He spins by the rail-edge and kicks loose
the gravel. This is like a sandstorm
he says, like the waves of an actual desert.

ICONOCLASTIC

Our Lord is tall and strong and tends his lambs. He faces west.
He holds a half-shredded staff in a hand held up by a vine.
Here are the girls in the churchyard holding hands, hanging leis
on Our Lady's neck, stacking them so her face purples and yellows
with the petals and pollen, the twine pressed on her lips.
Here are the boys loitering, half-drunk from Gem Clear, splayed
on the side of the ridge, praying the Creed by heart. In the crèche,
in the copra husk cradle, Our Lord's eyes are crossed and bleached,
glazed, specked gray from the salt and the rain that drains through
his plastered hair, his skull, the split bridge of his nose.
Here the columns are Roman and ragged. They chip when touched.
If it is true, then when the cisterns crack and the clouds part
from where a man once roped the moon from the sky, he will come
in a canoe glistening at the grains, with cloaks and nets overflowing.
The sweetest water will fall and flood the ruts from the upland homes,
and higher yet to the peaks and plateaus, to the land left
from the last wounds, from the holy men. Here the rocks
that built the road recede. They tilt and pull apart. They scatter
to the mangrove swamp where the jagged root-knives divide the fish
from their bodies. The women we love sing to the trade winds,
to the stems picked clean of fruit. The steeple's bottom beam
bends and the metal twists and tangles dead leaves into knots.
The women we love wear dresses that puff and press in the wind,
their shapes imprinted in the pillar grooves and the Cathedral grass,
the gusts curving through holes in the walls where windows
once cast the saints in the churchyard, in the village—*Anthony,*
Stephen. They could be the third lungs, our lost songs.

EXPLANATION

The broken-throated sound was not this boy
almost cutting his brother's head off, it was his mother
burning herself with animal fat. The oil melted

her forehead. She cleans the bishop's sacristy, boils
his rice. She washes his face when his hands won't stop
shaking. Her boy cuts down his bananas, spears

his fish. He tries on collars and rings and padlocks the gate
when the compound power cuts again and again.
The high title men swear he doesn't speak well

and can't count. It can be explained by her hair
teased out from a rock the night she walked on someone's land,
someone's grave. The wrong woman found her hair

and cut the strands, singed the braids so they curled
and smoked, shifted the mother's uterus
to the throat. Her cousins cut her bra and rubbed her

with coconut oil. They say the dead man's face
marks her womb and always will.
Now the mother's veins stick out like trails

and animal fat covers her face with heat
and blood. When she screams the women grinding
copra down the road remember the voice, the mother

who slept in a room next to the bishop
in case he needed help holding the Eucharist.
They remember she screamed the year the mountain fell.

It sounded like a woman ready to be a mother.
The boy came with no father and her uncles stopped
speaking. They gave their mangoes away

to the pigs chained by the shore.
The boy's fingers rot the scales off blue-fins
and mackerels. In mass, he swings the censer

and the incense stink stays. He reeks of it days later,
like a body badly oiled. The girls still young enough
to run naked hold their breath. The woman's face

looks sad. The place where she should cry is raw
and the flesh shiny. This is a place a ghost would go
if it wanted anything to do with her.

STORMSIDE

I

From the Baptist station static blurs the FM signal
distant and alien, almost unheard in certain inland huts
and abandoned quarries, but still comes the first word
of the trident-guided blast, the manic gale and monsoon,
the fomented gloom in the name of Cain, silver-haired
and spiked in the eye, cauterized and clutching
undertow rush, the brimstone storm
with its starved mouth jawing the reef rock
brittle and bringing the ocean boulders to dust,
the bleak-eyed thing streaking to the deadened end
of the sky, horizon's swelling fade, the knife-tipped
rogue wave, cut from the stone-money pass of Yap,
or could it be Guam the word says, the sin-rich strip,
the Hilton-high plague thumping a plaqued and salted heart,
ghosted to life like some secondhand nuke
or hydrogen-shroom, or slit from the crumbled condo
walls, pressed and tossed, tunneled to Saipan's busted sewers
and overgrown bunkers, plunging and glowing with the half-dead
glittering lights, trenched from plate to plate in the under-earth
slush, the magmatic pulse pouring a beat from the broken surface
to the seafloor dark. The word keeps coming. In its warped loop
the word rings, and there's a strange chill, a muggy film
that hangs green and loosens the knots on the bamboo beams
holding the huts to the ground. And the road brims
with believers, or men wanting to believe
in whatever prayer stalls the boats, whatever clears the night
of a warring moon jarring the sea free.

II

The grade school girls leave their slippers swinging
from power lines and scattered in the churchyard.

The woman who sells herself moves on her own,
goes quiet up the hill where her mother hangs clothes

to dry or sits alone, waiting for someone to walk by
and save her. On the widest stretch of the road

the truck beds fill until back-fat bulges over the sides
and the tires sag. Here are the gold-teeth girls

and the red-fingered boys watching the pallets
flatten under their feet, the unwed women pinned

to the back window, barely holding the handrails, afraid
of nothing, the worried fathers watching the whitecaps

rise, the half-black girls who grew up in the Gilberts,
never knowing the words of the sacred tongues, the voices

of the holy men. From the front of the truck, one boy
climbs through the window to the roof of the cab,

standing and then stomping the metal concave,
his head bowed to miss the trees. There are leaves

he balls in his hands. There are branches he breaks.

III

On the high ground, the compounds of Sapuk,
in the cast iron Catholic barricades shuttered
from all sides, in the makeshift shelter lit dimly

from a battery sitting on a piece of particle board,
wires bare and almost glowing, the women draw
their fans up and down and side to side, making the sign

of the cross, cooling the necks of their sons and their sisters,
the other women bent over against the wall, singing.
Give us what is right and just and good for all men.

And the word is there in the one working speaker,
the treble turning the bellow tinny, the hypnotic buzz
skipping from syllable to syllable, but still coming clear.

Who will be your keeper when the shadows ripple and flutter
up the back-way paths through the wire-windows and louvers,
stripping the ground red to clay? And what if the shore rolls

itself in a wrecking ball and flattens the mountain
on its climb to the sun? The white priest says there's more
than the sound it will make when it rises and falls and comes

again. There's the love of the Lord and the great hope
of a side-wind, a tilted axis bending southbound, a torrid shift
in the sea and the reef, a divide in the tide. And who wouldn't see

the grace in his words? Who wouldn't believe the truth
bearing down like some fearsome saber in the jungle?
It's worth the wait to watch the parted clouds,

the spreading cirrus shading the trees a darker green.
And when the mass begins in the one cemented room
two altar boys mimic the wind with the incense

they burn and then bow to the left. They bow to the right
where the bread sits unblessed, where there are women
whose noses touch the ground when they pray.

There is nothing to be said about the sky. There is nothing,
the word says, to stop this talk of the water,
of a light shining through the hinges of the door.

III

RESTORE

In the beginning the whale loses track of the channel
and catches the underside of its body on the reef.
Its fat leaks from a gash and melts from the tops
of rocks into the water. The men spearing fish see birds
swooping and floating, some with bits in their beaks.
The bigger waves stretch the fins and the men drop anchor
and for the first time see the eyes open and close.
The mouth bites to breathe and the torn flesh
drapes the surface, tinting reddish and then a darker
kind of blue. One man wants to scream and touches
the mouth with the back of his hand and one man slides
his bandanna into the wound. The whale is strong
and when it breathes turns the rocks to their clean sides,
away from the algae. The men wedge ropes and wait
for a good wave, for the right rush to come and wash
to shore. In the back, by the tail, where the water
is deeper and the current thicker, the strongest man
stands and pushes what he can, and on the third try
the whale shakes its body free and into the channel.
On the western beach the men's sons stand stoic
and watch the rods of the spine, the lifted fins, the body
they've only seen drawn in the sand. They climb
trees and knock the fruit with their feet to bring
the village elders and sisters, the women who've heard
and have their hair down, banging tin cans, stripping
from their tops, thumping their chest bones,
the boys slashing tree branches and tying rope
to rebar posts. And when the men come they cut shapes
in their thighs, lines like the fins flapping futile on the shore,
and they circle the whale and watch as it rocks in place,
half its body coated with sand and cloth-like leaves

gone grainy in the sun, the low tide beach becoming small,
the men grazing the skin with their blades, and the village
crowding closer and rubbing its hands together
when the knives begin to sing and rise and divide.

THE MIDDLE DAYS

In daylight, you're swarmed by flies. They land
on your skin where sand and salt has turned
to film. There could be worse things.

You see the compounds light up the shoreline,
the shacks with generators and good wicks.
The picked-over bags of trash caught

in a coral bed close to the fiberglass boats.
The high waves frame the water white,
and the clouds drift below the foam

with wind that hasn't come here in months.
Your son's face is broken into small squares
by the wire-grate. The light through

the thatch speckles his cheeks and his jaw-
bone slides apart when the leaves are blown
thin. He's there alone wedging unripened

mango, peeling the green skin with a dull knife.
He will unchain the chicken cage and walk
the wheelbarrow back and forth to spread

husks and dried shells and dropped flecks
of meat. You watch the peak of Tol, the hills
that come together between Uman and Fefan

and the mangrove trees sagging the shores
closer together. The current could pull you away.
The banana plants growing from the hedge

are bent and dragging, flooded, almost dying.
The driftwood trunks are wet and half-shaded.
You watch the bamboo poles arc with your weight.

The grains stretch and the joints widen.
When you move, they nearly break.

EXPLANATION

The brothers do as they're told and strew plumeria
blossoms on their father's grave and leave
in the canoe with loose dirt and the hammer
he made from mangrove. The god of moving sand
forms in the shadow of the crab shell
on the seafloor, and the oldest of their mothers
sees the truth coming between the ribs of a yellowfin,
where the saltwater and crushed lime settles
and turns the red meat white, and who are they
to disagree with the movement the paddles make
when the wind picks branches off the high trees
on Tol? And who are the mothers to speak now
since the brothers have burned the dolphin fins
and spread the ashes in every pocket of clear water?
The god of turtle eggs walks perfectly
from sky to sky and Sirius leans and glares
and bleeds half-blue in the breadfruit season.
The brothers say the last meteor is proof
that the truth can come from the moons
of Mercury, from the burning dots of light
swirling over the stern. The god of the first wave
darkens their skin until something they couldn't imagine
marks their bodies, something they know
from the water. They invent the face
their father made when he came off the boat
alone, empty-handed. With a knife, the brothers
form the cheeks from the spine of a fish,
and from their own eyes, they make his,
and the movement passes over their hands,
two molds growing hard and taking shape.

SYNTHESIZE

At the cathedral, village drifters scaffold the wall
and claw at what's loose or soon to fall
from shambled archways, the easy break of concrete
off the window-ledge where stained glass blazes blue
to seaside trash fires, to the causeway, the crawl
of flatbeds blaring sirens from bullhorn mics, my father
and I slumped in our seats, New Year's Eve,
revving the engine, bumping the system
we taped to a spare tire. The bass hum blurs
in the mud flaps, the fizzle of treble, Chuukese reggae
clicking a simple beat, the secondhand Marley laze,
steel-drum thump, the synth hi-hat's perfect clap,
seamless from track to track, speakers heaving,
nearly spent, the sound we hope is heard in coral beds
molded like knives. My father rolls a cigarette and burns
three dots on his arm and holds my hand to touch him
where skin used to be, like a constellation
he says, like satellites. This is how a man feels,
he tells me as he bleeds, as he blows smoke
through cracked lines in the dash.
At the bridge we stop to throw rocks at boats
sticking up in the low tide. On their rusted tanks
the woozy boys drum a beat with sheet metal
and spatulas, mangrove sticks and copra shells,
gas cans strapped to their ankles, stray power lines
whipped in rhythm to the ground. We sing,
my father and I, steady from breath to breath,
holding long notes, his voice a key I search for
in the whoosh of the trees bending in the wind.

THE TIDE LIGHT

The sleep we have under a tin roof.
The silence we stole from standing birds on a sand bar,
picking the cheeks of a fish. How the hands
return insistently, the limp weight, wind
growing thin in shy turns of the head,
the dream's lucid vines dried in thatch-weave
beneath us. What the moon means
in its dimpled trance, wild green light
remade in the tilt and bend of our bodies,
trapped space tunneled from under us,
the dream reflecting what comes and goes
from gathering clouds over Tol, growing
in the slow slide of sand crabs, the remembered hush
of palm leaves, heat-streaks cutting the sky
in two. Imagine the leaps we take in the Southern Cross,
its constellating angles, the navigated current
dipping clean from star to star. Imagine sails
becoming full, showing their threaded, skin-thin
lines of light, and the dream becoming more
than the ticking sound the turtle makes on the bare rock
of the reef or the rush of the ocean floating a wave
over its hidden head, lifting the webbed feet,
the faded shell, the worn water breaking the surface.

EXPLANATION

It will take a good fight to bring her back
and the chief orders his men to call
her with conch shells, even if it means love

or staying on the beach when the sand hardens.
There's a chance she'll float like Olofat
who spat blood and broke himself

into an archipelago. There's a chance
she drank the sweet water in Tol
and poured her body out as a spring.

There's the half-caste joke about the men
who left the lighthouse years ago.
No one can discuss sunsets or the fiberglass

of the boat or the story about her breasts
bloating later in the shape of an island,
into real rock. A bulletin goes out

and the boys climb trees for signals.
It could be days she stays huddled there,
and the oddsmaker on Saipan

places his faith in the fish she might spear.
Big deal some say, remember when the cliff
had imprints of hands left from the landslide.

There's the chance she's stuck
in a tunnel of coral or torn to tufts
and in that case a boy could start killing

the pigs. She left the Mortlocks at night
and now the women cover the fences
with fronds and start with the baskets.

There's a hope she'll drift again as scraps
of land, as the upper half of a woman's body,
the curve of sand in her neck.

GROTESQUERIE

I love the bloated women stricken
in the bent-beamed meetinghouse,
the veiny figures static-stretched,
split and sprawled, the wood grains

gripping the bellows, the bodies
soggy in the whole heat of breezeless
light, the shameless scab-lines
pocked to patchwork and termite silt,

the side board bending, core-cut
and varicose-corked in the screw supports
and the rust-marked thigh sores,
the saddle-skid flapped and cracked

and can't I love the stuffed mouth
spewing, the rubbed raw ridges brimming
to the ledge, the creature-beached
boredom corroded and canker-laced,

kin-coarse, cupping rice and Spam,
slabbing themselves to boorish sheets,
to knotted bulges of breast, ripples
of wrecked angles under the jaws,

the sedentary skin, rashed and reeking,
the flesh-rinds I'd pick to bits
between my fingers? I love to watch them
roll, unfold, go smooth for the first time.

BLACKOUT

The night the Chuukese girl hanged herself
with a Nintendo cord, we fucked

in the Saramen Academy parking lot,
behind the tinted glass and the overhang

retaining walls. It was good like this,
the engine heat and the broken-open seats

of the Hi-Lux, the torn cushion
under us, matted like the hair

of fathers, like the built-up clumps
of bare ice after a blackout, turning

to snow. And so we stuck our hips
out and rolled them with strands

and sheets, into dunes breaking
over bones, into the split limbo

between us, and in our hands
we made flakes of golden cowries

and 3-D imprints of sand dollars,
crystals dangled over the earlobes,

the streaked lines of shells gone soft
and insignificant, condensed to gray

on our cheeks like claw marks.
They barely touched us. We sank

to where the welds drew lines,
and a kneeling figure leaned

in shadows of ashes on the dash,
and whatever was still white

hung from the window,
and whatever felt cold there,

whatever opened the doors
and ripped the seat to its hinges

and spring-edges and faux-leather folds,
we left threaded and thin,

plowed out and disappeared,
and after that, we left.

KATARI

After hours of strict respect
from the man who loves me
for a time each year, I enter
the cookhouse with a mirror
and a shard of louver
to loosen two teeth of a turtleshell comb
from my forehead.
It was a gift to me, the comb.
The skilled threadwork left me
leaning. The respect that ran for me
now runs from me and I lay
down my arms. From a line
by the road a hanging skirt drifts
upward. I was not always loved
so heavily, so accepted
into the rhythm of survival,
so stalled in a bloodline
which bends for no one,
not even the beautiful.
In the right darkness, I go
to the top of the hill
where Americans listen to all
the sounds the ocean
never makes. I want to clean them
from their happiness until the flies
gather where fruit splits
its sweetness. I want my shore
to teach them the smallness
of a flower grove, a shadow
which sways into the water
and lessens.

EXPLANATION

She dives off the dock alone on her lightest day
of bleeding and even the leaves in the guava trees
shake free, even the mangrove branches crack
and clutter the shore. She breaks the waves clear

and turns a funnel of foam still, her song lost
in clouds of spray. Her mother wants to stop it
in the taro patch, twist the roots and squeeze saltwater
through raw cracks and veins that keep

leaking to the mud below. The clan must be saved
somehow. The sisters bury the rotting breadfruit
and wait for it to sweeten and run. The undertow
pulls shadows from the surface to the seafloor,

moving in blocks with schools of yellow-fins.
The aunties dry the seaweed caught in the coral.
They want to cover her piece by piece, heal her.
The brothers do what they can with dust

they rub off a tree they won't name. They take it
to heart when she grows sick and pats their cheeks
with the back of her hand. She wants a shift
in the night-wind, a distance to rush through

the way a fishbone threads a palm. She wants
to massage herself with swordgrass and bent stems,
to wait for harvest to swell and cleanse her.

CONVERT

In what meant more than love
she walked with him in daylight,
her hip grazing his on the way to the grave
of his host father, where they prayed ten beads
in English. In LA they camped on beaches
where surfers watched her swim
and said she was beautiful and perfect,
her hair full and upstanding, her wet skirt
like the imprint of some jungle sun.
They took taxis and followed the sidewalks
and window-shopped on streets
that looked like landing strips
or church-lots she said, low tide fields
of broken coral. He gave her ten dollars a day
to move through the city but still they kissed
only in darkness, in her secret tongue,
with their eyes squinting shut,
in theatres and squatter spots, lost in parks
where the lamps flickered off
when it rained. It was the shine in her body
he loved, and though she wanted to have him
on the mat she'd woven from hibiscus,
in smoothed-out sand, he said nothing
could ever be enough and wanted to leave
for smaller towns with border jumpers
selling rotten guava and four-dollar cans
of copra water. Sometimes she'd let him
unbraid her hair and tease split ends
in his hands. In the late heat of summer
with the Pacific fading behind them,
the beach empty except for gulls

picking at bread, she let him run his fingers
close to her head, over the paler parts
he loved to touch, against the scalp
where he traced the letters of his name.

RECOLLECT

There was a hideaway
made of cement and bamboo.
There was a clean cloth,
a bag of betelnut, a bottle of yeast
and sugar-water four-hours old.
There was a flashlight covered
and dimming. There were shadows
on the walls broken and rippled
to pieces. There was a place
where you made me close
for the first time and bent my arm
to the point of breaking
like I wanted, like I made you do
for the honor of my father's village.
You undid your hair
to cover my chest. I remember
a lit butt pressed to my wrist,
fishbones threaded through my fingers.
There were names we made
for our low tide souls.
I wanted to finish you.
I wanted to move and turn you
from your quiet language,
but you held your breath.
You wanted to be stronger
and last. There was a time
when men knew how to die
in this village, when to jump
from the ridge with their jaws set,
their faces carved
like canoes that came here

71

when the land was just rocks
and sun. There was smoke
and there was blood.
There was the heat coming
above the reef at dawn.
It was like a plumeria you said,
a real blossom swelling, a spot
of white rising in the center,
spreading and taking hold.

FUNEREAL

The women wrap their dresses under their shins.
Their voices leave the meetinghouse for tree-beds
and cracked sheet metal roofs. Plumerias cover

the floor where a basket of money sits, where my father
shakes hands. Braided fronds loosen on the fence
by the road, and girls who knew my brother well

crouch by the wall looking in, their hands red
from plucking the rusted wire of a window.
I'm watching my mother fan the face and touch

the mouth with oil. I'm watching my cousins
who wear collared shirts pass a bag of betelnut
between them. My oldest uncle leans on a pipe,

his arms bulging from the sleeves. The generator clicks in
and shadows fade from unpounded nails
and sagging beams. I'm told they found him

two compounds from here, by the dying breadfruit tree,
by the house of a girl he went with, a spot he swept
the leaves from. In the waiting line aunties ask for plates,

for the bin of pig meat. They ask if I've had enough.
I remember shoving him to the edge of his truck
in front of my father and bruising his knee.

He slashed a V into my arm and ran off
to carve his canoe. And on the tables, flies pull bits
of fish from bones left by men I'm told are uncles.

I've never met them. Men file through with bags of rice.
Boys sit by the door or wait in picked-apart cars
alive with tapioca growing from the engine

or through springs under the seats,
where even the floor is rotted out and blooming.

SCROLL

There are hymnals stuck in potholes
praising the miracle of the sparrow.
There is a boy asking the chief

for mercy, for a last chance to live
again in the village, with no war at his back.
There are names we drew on our arms

with battery acid. There is a Baptist placard
praying for abstinence, the red letters faded
to pink, signs on ships with Japanese words

for *tuna* and *trespass* passing through
en route to Guam. There are words
the chief writes with the end of a dried root,

into a patch of mud he made red
by singing the sacred language.
There are words the boy says

only under his breath. When Barack won
we loved him even before we knew
his voice. We loved him in his Hawaiian shirts

and hung the black and white papers
on the meetinghouse walls until they curled up
and fell. We practiced his five syllables, chanted

and waved dry palms down the road.
There is the word *tong* which means love
but what do we say to the boy

who might as well be dead?
We say *good evening* but mean
where are you going?

There are chants meaning war
and there are prayers we sing
when the bread has been blessed.

There's a dance we do in our red cloth
with our hands spinning to a trance.
The chief takes a hand to the boy's head

and carries the spirit to the mangrove swamp,
but where does the current send him then?
Where does the trade wind lift him?

There are clouds over the ridge at Wittapong
breaking apart in green strands, from village
to village, sometimes in rain

sometimes in darkness. There are names
for how the dust rises up and catches
in the trees. If we could dream him back
we would.

ACKNOWLEDGMENTS

Grateful acknowledgment is made to the following magazines whose editors offered these poems their original publication:
Alaska Quarterly Review, Atlas Review, Boston Review, Blackbird, Cincinnati Review, Connotation Press, Copper Nickel, Drunken Boat, Fourteen Hills, Grist, Handsome Journal, Hayden's Ferry Review, The Iowa Review, The Journal, Linebreak, Many Mountains Moving, Miracle Monocle, Night Train, Nimrod, The Normal School, Notre Dame Review, Poet Lore, Rhino, Slate, Sycamore Review, Two Weeks: A Digital Anthology of Contemporary Poetry, and*Witness.*

I am grateful for the support of my family and friends, who have helped me grow as a person and as a writer. I would like to thank Seth Abramson, Katie Asher Halquist, Quan Barry, Kai Carlson-Wee, Brittany Cavallaro, Katie Childs, Brett DeFries, Louisa Diodato, Robin Ekiss, Ted Genoways, Peter Halquist, Fran Hezel S.J., Amaud Jamaul Johnson, Barb and Dave Kalscheur, Lisa Kalscheur, Ruth Kalscheur, Jesse Lee Kercheval, James Longenbach, Tyler Martin, Tim McDonald, Chris Pearson, Jacques J. Rancourt, Nancy Reddy, Aaron Schloer, Ron Wallace, Eliot Khalil Wilson, my community of volunteers on Weno, the students and staff at Xavier High School-Micronesia and Bradbury's Coffee where most of this book was written and revised.

Josh Kalscheur's poems have appeared in *Slate, Boston Review, The Iowa Review, jubilat* and *Best New Poets 2013*, among others. He lives in Madison, WI where he teaches English classes at both UW-Madison and Madison College.

Publication of this book was made possible by grants and donations. We are also grateful to those individuals who participated in our 2014 Build a Book Program. They are:

Nickie Albert
Michele Albright
Whitney Armstrong
Jan Bender-Zanoni
Juanita Brunk
Ryan George
Michelle Gillett
Elizabeth Green
Dr. Lauri Grossman
Martin Haugh
Nathaniel Hutner
Lee Jenkins
Ryan Johnson
Joy Katz
Neal Kawesch
Brett Fletcher Lauer & Gretchen Scott
David Lee
Daniel Levin
Howard Levy
Owen Lewis
Paul Lisicky
Maija Makinen
Aubrie Marrin
Malia Mason
Catherine McArthur
Nathan McClain
Michael Morse
Chessy Normile
Rebecca Okrent
Eileen Pollack

Barbara Preminger
Kevin Prufer
Soraya Shalforoosh
Alice St. Claire-Long
Megan Staffel
Marjorie & Lew Tesser
Boris Thomas
William Wenthe